light traveling over

from equations l

DISTANCE
LEARNING

Series

ert Scott

Advisory Editors	Nancy Eimers, Mark Halliday, William Olsen, J. Allyn Rosser
Assistant to the Editor	Rebecca Beech
Assistant Editors	Allegra Blake, Jenny Burkholder, Becky Cooper, Rita Howe Scheiss, Nancy Hall James, Kathleen McGookey, Tony Spicer
Editorial Assistants	Melanie Finlay, Pamela McComas
Business Manager	Michele McLaughlin
Fiscal Officer	Marilyn Rowe

The New Issues Press Poetry Series is sponsored by the College of Arts and Sciences, Western Michigan University.

First Edition, 1998.

ISBN: 0-932826-61 X (cloth)
ISBN: 0-932826-26 8 (paper)

Library of Congress Cataloging-in-Publication Data:
Sorby, Angela 1965–
Distance Learning / Angela Sorby
Library of Congress Catalog Card Number (97-069532)

Art Direction:	Tricia Hennessy
Design:	Christina Render
Production:	Paul Sizer
	The Design Center, Department of Art
	College of Fine Arts
	Western Michigan University
Printing:	Bookcrafters, Chelsea, Michigan

DISTANCE LEARNING

ANGELA SORBY

FOREWORD BY MEKEEL McBRIDE

New Issues Press

WESTERN MICHIGAN UNIVERSITY

Distance Learning is for Janet and Evan Sorby.

Contents

Part Three: Garden of Forks

Part Four: Distance Learning

Foreword

Angela Sorby is, in many respects, like a Sufi dancer who stops just long enough to send back news from her brilliant spiralings into the heart of things. Where you start in a Sorby poem is not where you end up, though everything connects. It's as if you've been shown how to reconcile San Francisco with Boston by unexpected meditations on a midwestern prairie. You can get here from there but, when you arrive, everything is changed. For instance, in "Timber Queen," you might think you're going to meet Sasquatch, the huge and elusive legendary beast of the Northwest, but when he finally shows up he turns out to be merely rat-sized. He carries a bunch of ferns to a former beauty queen who has clearly been doing some eating since the last pageant. And so the poem turns into a wry commentary on exaggeration and leaves us musing on myth's misshapen but strangely appealing children.

Sorby's is the poetry of fast-paced, brilliant connections, links and losses made manifest with impeccable and beguiling music. Her use of the colloquial is as crisp and infinity-tinged as a Hockney swimming pool. A quirky, intelligent humor often informs and reframes her most difficult subjects. Language, here, is always wry and energetic. Sometimes she enlists the tense delight of piled-on rhyme, as in the opening of "Synchronized Swimming":

> How did decay work its way into the theater of water,
> the Green Lake Aqua Stadium that was clear as chlorine
> all through the fifties when Marilyns, Sues and Doreens
>
> formed a human hula hoop of blues and greens?

Other times her language glows quiet and soft with the risky pleasure of picking up the elusive fingerprints of paradox. Then, the poetry's more likely to resort to some mesmerizing dance of assonance, slant rhyme, alliteration—the kind of motion that might lure a cobra right out of darkness for a dangerous kiss.

In fact, language or lack of it is often a concern in Sorby's work. The book's gorgeous first poem, "Glossolalia," concerns itself with the consequences of ecstatic utterances. A suburban neighbor tries to beguile the narrator into religion by praying in tongues. As she begins praying, her voice becomes "a plant/ forcing out blooms:// cinnamon spikes/ bees in the nightshade,// a foxglove fugue." This inspired and untranslatable music "veers" suburbia into "a garden/ overrun with wilderness." By the end of the poem, the narrator asks, "How could I not feel// Christ's knuckles rap/ hard on my heart?"— a question tempered by preceding lines in which the narrator admits she's "fourteen and close// enough to touch Rae Anne's/ braids, her bangs,// her birch white hair part."

This may be as much feeling someone else's God knocking on her heart as it is a clear awareness of whose throat the music's emerging from. However you choose to read it, the fact remains that any good dictionary will yield up one origin of the word "God" to be "voice" which suggests that divinity of a sort might conceivably be linked with the ability to sing.

Distance Learning, itself, is a renegade garden, rife with fierce music. Sorby's poems wake you up with surprising knocks to the heart. Music's everywhere here. It's a music that has learned its scales and suffered with the strict, frozen-spined metronome and now has earned its right to sassy jazz.

In "Kate Fox," a more complex look at language, Kate, a medium in the 1800s charged with fraud, admits that though she claimed to be talking to the dead, in fact she learned at an early age "to crack my toe-bones until they echoed/ like raps from beyond the grave./ Soon my body was a bag of tricks." She devised this fraudulent mediumship to liberate herself from the mindless work of endless sewing. By the end of the poem Fox admits, "I was the whole/ heavenly host. I was as good as it gets." She speaks with irony, like a shyster shaking an empty sack in front of an unhappy customer. Still, a peculiar truth emerges, crackling with irony. Where else could the voices of the dead exist except inside the harmed and struggling bodies of those still alive?

Later, we encounter a man who claims to have given up language altogether, in "The Man Without A Middle." When his heart feels too con-stricted, he removes it and buries it under a "maze of foxgloves." (The poem does not mention this, but the heart stimulant digitalis is made from the foxglove plant, so it's interesting to note that he's buried his heart where it has a chance of being healed.) He then fills his empty rib cage with birds because they "ask nothing" of him and "cannot be bothered with words." The aviary-hearted fellow laments, "So many things are more central than love." Still, he cannot help but admit that one of these things is the woman "in the park near the Gare St-Lazare . . . who scatters the bread." And, of course, a kindness that translates into bread is just about as close to love as you can get.

Here, among other things, you will find this man with a heart made out of birds; Emily Dickinson, suddenly appearing as a twin to Marilyn Monroe; a UFO poem that turns out to be a searing, clear look at racism. This is a book of marvels and wonders, spangled bridges and blessedly safe parachutes. It is the poet herself who scatters a magic bread in the giving of these rich poems.

Mekeel McBride

Acknowledgments

Grateful acknowledgment is made to the editors and publishers of the following publications, in which these poems first appeared:

ACM: "Glossolalia"
The Baffler: "Teen Idol, Found OD'd"
Brooklyn Review: "Timber Queen," "Gold Rush"
Kansas Quarterly: "Museum Piece"
Lactuca: "The Man without a Middle"
New Virginia Review: "Life Ring"
North American Review: "Weather at Ten"
Poet & Critic: "Gossip"
Spoon River Quarterly: "Yoga," "Uses of Enchantment"
Sycamore Review: "Distance Learning," "Antarctica"
Third Coast: "Empire Builder," "Kate Fox,"
    "Land of Lincoln"
Thirteenth Moon: "A Diary in the Strict Sense of the Term,"
    "Doing Theory"
William and Mary Review: "Storm Porch, at Thirteen"
Wisconsin Review: "Shopping at the Bon Marché"

"Museum Piece" was reprinted in *The Nation* and in *Best American Poetry 1995,* Richard Howard and David Lehman, eds., (NY: Simon & Schuster, 1995).

I would also like to acknowledge, with gratitude, the support of the MAD-M Collective (Dawn Marlan, Maureen McLane, Mary Lass Stewart), the Centrum Foundation, Alane Rollings, Christopher Roth, and the late Nelson Bentley.

Part One: Roof of the World

Glossolalia

Rae Anne Redfield
is dying for me

to convert to Pentecostal
Christianity,

so one summer day
she prays in tongues,

her voice a plant
forcing out blooms:

cinnamon spikes,
bees in the nightshade,

a foxglove fugue.
My parents' patio

turns hot as lungs,
unsticks from the grid

of level lawns,
and veers into a garden

overrun with wilderness.
I'm fourteen and close

enough to touch Rae Anne's
braids, her bangs,

her birch white hair part.
How could I not feel

Christ's knuckles rap
hard on my heart?

Yoga

It's 1970, the year
before I learned to read.
My mother's in lotus
on an orange towel
trying to breathe through her right nostril
which is the "nostril of purification."
I watch her from the rocker
and remember last night's dream:
clouds shaped like blades
cut the tops off our birches.
My mother's hair is blackbirds
bursting out of a pie.
She got the Lapp gene,
while my hair's limp and faint
as lefse. My mother labors
to control her pulse.
Her clavicle jumps.
Her blood makes waves.
I know if it weren't for me
my mother would levitate
beyond the Cascade snow line
and over the roof of the world,
and she says that soon
by murmuring shantih
as a mantra
she will end the war
that's been everywhere,
even inside of us,
since I was born.

Timber Queen

Olympic Peninsula, Washington State

When the Sasquatch
finally stumbles into Forks,
he's tiny, the size of a grainy
newspaper clip.
Lynn, the 1973 Timber Queen,
spots him from her perch
on the blue porch.
As she stands to squint,
her fat feels wrong,
like someone's mother's
hand-me-down sweater.
He might be a rat
from the town dump
but he walks upright
and clutches a mess
of maidenhair ferns.
She always knew
he'd come too late to carry her
into the Hoh rainforest
where nothing dries
so nothing dies completely:
the robin's rotted wing lifts up
as huckleberries sprout
between its bones.
When the Sasquatch
finally stumbles into Forks,
no one runs for a camera
or rings the Enquirer.
Lynn gives him a bowl
of dog chow soaked in water.
The sun is so bright
it ought to be warmer.

Museum Piece

Now that your ship is ready, Susan, that hoop skirt sailing
down the aisle, a milk-white frigate of bound tits,

I must say congrats, you're "of age," he's nice and all that,
but I in my blue satin sausage skin want to stand

up and rage because there's been an end to courting
psychos by hitchhiking on Aurora, an end to splitting

one filched beer on the overpass in the dead of night.
Then, you smelled like a hundred hours of babysitting:

Pabulum and cannabis. You'd steal my homework in a snap.
You were unwholesome, Susan. When I throw rice today,

I want to throw firecrackers and globs of canned frosting.
I want to throw COREY'S SLUG AND SNAIL DEATH in honor

of the toxic lawns in our parents' suburb. I want to jump up
during the ceremony, grab you and drag you back to our moral

vacuum, to watch your hair over and over like a blue
video: the way its long straight darkness swallows light.

But I shut up and grip my carnations. So this is how jinxed
card decks, blood feud bullets and lava-soaked cats end

up at the museum under glass. So we didn't O.D. or get
        slashed,
and now it's safe as school, it's folded up like a gossip note,

pale, pocket-sized, nothing that'd blow you away, this past.

Land of Lincoln

That's where Lyle Wilson went, wearing his Mariners
baseball cap. In 1979 he was drinking tequila by a paper shack
near Bothell, Washington, when he got killed by a car
that didn't stop. The driver drove right into the Reagan
revolution, leaving Lyle Wilson, a boy who was no longer
human, to escape like smoke wafting out of a stovepipe
hat. The afterlife is bare as Illinois: the Land of Lincoln,

south of Chicago, where farms flatten to grey as if a spray
of ash has fallen. I'm loath to drive through,
even with the windows rolled up, but I did it once,
en route to St. Louis. The towns were not true towns:
just Burger Kings, and houses with their doors nailed shut.
No wrestling teams were practicing in the dark
and windowless gyms. In the Land of Lincoln, everything
turns into him: he's a tow truck, a tire store,
a bank, a school, a canister of logs, and a national park.

There is no heartland except in the heart: it is a single
apple, the red start of two or three trees. It is not Illinois,
where the prairie root systems are uprooted. Is it weird to lust
after the dead? Sometimes I picture Lyle, luminous in his skin.
I wait for his pulse until it beats in my wrist. In American
gothic novels the heroines aren't really afraid of ghosts.
No, they're afraid of ironing: the board, the sheets
and pillowcases, the flatness, the Midwestern

flatness.

The Quiet Brother

for Sten

When we lived in the house
beyond all bus lines,
the TV brewed a tempest
in its tiny glass tubes,
and Jim shot a dart,
downing a big cat,
on Mutual of Omaha's
Wild Kingdom.
No snow leopards stole
a glance at you, Sten,
through the picture window,
not even when it snowed,
though the kitchen bulb stared
with its one good eye
like a predator at the zoo.
It stared the limitless
sledding air right out of you,
until you were warm
as wheat toast:
    eat this, it's good for you.
You wanted to stay
outside with your sled
behind the Inglewood
Golf Course shed,
hungry, hood down,
teeth peaceably closed,
and watch the stars spit
unlinked syllables
of light, nonsensically
burning hot and cold.

Darwin in the Cascade Mountains

An angel reads in the A-frame.
  Snow falls, big as wolf paws.
   One snowshoer bursts in, panting.

The angel turns to cake.
  Gravity holds down the shingles.
    If levity fell in flakes,

it would raise the roof
 and all the firs into the sky.
   Ann, the tired snowshoer,

teaches math and often dreams
  in algebra. Her husband died
    of a brain tumor in November.

His radiation didn't take,
  but the A-frame radiates
    with his boots, his time

release capsules, his camping
 lantern, his tumbler. The dead
   give off heat, like sugar.

The *Voyage of the Beagle*
  lies open upside down
    on the floor, a tiny tent

of sea plants culled from the coast
   of Tierra del Fuego:
     Having kept a large tuft

in a basin of water,
  when it was dark I found
    that as often as I rubbed a part

of the branch, the whole
  became phosphorescent
    with a strong light.

The book's spine is cracked.
  Do readers leave a residue,
    like salt crystals in a shell?

If X = sea plants and Y= firs,
  can Ann dream a landscape
    where she snowshoes back

into the wilderness alone,
  under an ocean of green, her muscles
    burning to keep her warm?

Storm Porch, at Thirteen

Neah Bay's blue-black waves
require the strength of a Hobie racer,
his gut a geoduck crouching and arching,
but it's October and everyone's brother
is working out indoors.
I eat saltines on the storm porch,
while my gerbil, Androcles,
runs circles of plastic din in his ball,

and I remember seawater drying
on my skin last summer:
see-through layers of seal spit, Canadian
oil, swimmer's sweat, how the small
of my back broke into a rash,
how one warm night a Hobie racer
spanned my waist with his hands
out on the aluminum pier,
and fear scattered salty under my halter,
until I prayed for barnacle knuckles
that could grind an escape tunnel
straight out of August,

into cold weather,
the silence of stacked saltines,
and the clatter of Androcles orbiting
over uneven floorboards.
Maybe the sea is better shorn
of Hobies. This glassed-in room
makes all the world windless—
with six rectangles of ocean,
one Adirondack chair,
and my own fingers parting
and twisting
my own hair.

Gold Rush

You find the Petrified Man
lodged under glass at the back
of Ye Olde Curiosity Shoppe,
a tourist trap on Puget Sound.
He is skinny, a cross
between Christ and a bat.
Tar pit, you figure,
or mummification in long johns.
No relatives bore him back
to a churchyard in Boston or Sweden.
His rib cage is sunken
but immaculate the way a mud flat
looks clean at dawn
before the first clam diggers.
His shell toughens,
exempt from the preacher,
foreclosure, locusts, a boyish
lover with transparent wrists,
whatever drove him
north to muck for gold.
A sign on the case
reads *do not touch,*
but you already feel weather
conditions in his country,
so close that your spine
matches the shoreline node for node,
but so far away that ferries float
there under different stars, under a big
dipper full of *what?*
       Not light, not water,
       not spit, not blood.

Part Two: Mesmer's Daughter

Kate Fox

Who became a professional medium after she
reported the "Hydesville rappings" of 1848, and
who later confessed to fraud.

When I was thirteen, I thought I would grow
pale as lace, forced to sew and sew
my brain into a filigree
of threads and holes. Then I learned

to crack my toe-bones until they echoed
like raps from beyond the grave.
Soon, my body was a bag of tricks,
a telegraphic alphabet: croaks, moans, clicks.

I wore black gloves and a veil wrapped
around my face like a wasp's nest.
I charged a dollar per deceased
and fifty cents for stillborn babies.

And what do you know? The spirits spoke,
rapping *shall we gather at the river*—
Do I wish I'd married a farmer
like my father, with burrs in his beard? No;

I cleared eight hundred bucks a year,
though the frontier of the dead was closed—
I moved like a pioneer into the deep
recesses of my knees and throat.

Knock-knock!
        Who's there?
                It was always me,
never an infant with coins on its lids,
never a fisherman caught in a net. I was the whole
heavenly host. I was as good as it gets.

Ekphrasis

*399. One might also say: surely the owner of the visual
room would have to be the same kind of thing as it is;
but he is not to be found in it, and there is no outside.*
—Ludwig Wittgenstein

In van Ruysdael's frozen landscape,
the trees are inflexible bones.
The river's lone skater

is short but long-shadowed.
Her last baby tooth is safe
in her pocket. Her molars

rest lightly together.
It's early March. Soon, sun-
light will crack the river

and cats will hiss
in the grass. The skater will burst
a button, and comb out

her red-brown braids. Soon,
but not now, no, never
quite now: the visual room

is a room without breath.
Framing's another
word for death,

and only under the ice
do fish without eyes
muscle out of the visible

and survive.

Earhart

Solid ground makes me sneeze.
Goodbye, juniper. Goodbye, wheat.
Goodbye, cat and collie fur.

I'm shedding germs, I'm skirting public
pools of polio. The sun dips low.
Kansas is rotting, its spires turning

to compost. I point my nose
towards the coast. My gears
smell an ocean of salt, zones

of frost and heat, wind shears
too fast to be mapped.
Ezekiel saw the wheels a-rolling—

but goodbye to all that.
Modernity deep-sixed heaven
so the night sky's abstract,

like the urban lights of New York or London,
each star the cigarette tip
of an exploding story,

and I always knew I belonged up here,
in the sprawl of the real
big city.

Jump-Rope

Miss Mary Mac, Mac, Mac
All dressed in black, black, black
With silver buttons, buttons, buttons
All down her back, back, back . . .

The photos in '50s albums
are edged in black

corners to keep them
pasted flat. In her prom

shot my mother's too buttoned
up to unbutton,

like Miss Mary Mac,
the jump-rope rhyme

girl who's nailed in a coffin.
How could my parents

pre-date me? I suspect
that the fifties were faked

like a mock turtleneck:
no arms, no torso, no heft.

Eisenhower, "Teenangel,"
fallout shelters:

it sounds like the junk
kids invent

when they're caught sneaking
home after hours.

If there's a real story,
it's written in cold war Korean,

in an alphabet shaped
like modular furniture.

Where have all
the hula hoops gone?

They've rolled back
into the dark garage,

leaving no proof
of purchase,

no body
at the center of the blur.

Her Likeness

I start re-reading Dickinson
and suddenly she's everywhere

like Warhol's Marilyns sporting
the blue lips of the dead.

I work in a pea-green cardigan,
but why whine? Dickinson, too,

is doomed to wearing the same old
outfit for hundreds of years,

no Oz shoes, no mother of pearl
nose stud, no boa brushing

the nerves on her neck—
only a ribbon pinned prim

like a pie prize under her chin.
Whale bone stays are the closest

she'll come to Moby Dick,
but that's close enough to stick

his ribs into her heart,
close enough to make her freeze,

harpooned by technologies
of light and exposure,

the black box, the hooded
daguerrotypist, his click, his closure.

Cosmos

The purple flowers,
    so light they can fly,
      are called *cosmos,*
  and they grow on skinny stalks,
    easily blown over.
Why were they still alive yesterday,
     a cold day in October,
        as we walked in the woods
           by the Carbon River,
        just us, mother and daughter?
    And over the cosmos, birches arched
      to make a hall,
    as if the outdoors were a house,
    and not a wild place.
But even our insides are wilderness:
    when she was pregnant with me,
one of my mother's kidneys
    started to grow cancer cells,
      the strangest of fish,
        barracuda spreading
         below her lowest rib.
      She had to leave it alone
    if she wanted me to live.
        I floated, oblivious, a tiny
          water lily.

      Finally, I was born,
    and then they cut out her kidney.
What is wild? A wolf is wild,
      but so is a kidney, and so is a walk
    in late October, along the Carbon River.
My mother and I can't talk, not really—
      we struggle and spit in the same
        sprung trap, our love and anger

monstrously meshed
like a *liger*, half-lion,
half-tiger.

Nell Kimball

My brother Orion lost a leg
at Shiloh, so they pushed him West

in a wheelbarrow,
begging for ash cakes

from farms along the Ohio.
I was fourteen when he came home,

but I already knew how to mix powder
from orris root, bergamot,

oil of lemon and cloves.
I painted my cheeks

theater-color: two red spots.
Oh, I was ignorant as grass,

falling for Orion's friend
Charlie, a soldier with one hand

who could play Yankee Doodle
on a hollow turkey bone.

No enemies fired on me,
so I lost my figure slowly,

turning pro and whoring
for ten years with the railroad.

Anatomy baffles me,
how fat fills out a woman's thighs,

how ear-drums sort tones,
but I know I altered bit by bit:

jeweled eyes, wire hips.
I wear Nell's shoes, her hair, her hat,

but I'm bloodless as wax
worked by Madame Tussaud:

my pulse beats, but it's counterfeit,
a burnt-nerve trick, a shadow,

like Orion's leg that itched and itched
after he lost it at Shiloh.

Shopping at the Bon Marché

I am not an ancient Egyptian, so I know
the mannequins won't come alive to weave
our winding cloths or guide us across water when we die.

I know they're remote as Cleopatra;
remote as Liz Taylor, the last Cleopatra, polishing off vodka
        deep in Virginia;
remote as my grandmother, riding up next to me
        on the escalator,

whose middle name I don't remember, or have never known.
This store is "fashion-forward" but windowless and weirdly
immune to history, like a pyramid's chamber,

no Lucky Lindy, no world wars, as if my grandmother and I
could wander for ages without aging until we found a moving
silver staircase to escalate us up and out, over the top

floor, into the dome, into the sky blue that the saleswoman
told us we ought to wear, because we have the same light
eyes behind the same light hair.

Else Says

We all smoked pipes
in the Danish Girl Scouts
and knitted into late afternoon,
sealed in a sun room
until we smelled identical
like lovers after sex.
The scent of Prince DK tobacco
sank into my skeins
as I miscounted inches
and dropped shoulder stitches.
Below us, on Esbjerg harbor barges,
women scraped the hearts and guts
out of fish. During breaks
they paced the deck,
rubbing cream into their hands.
We were too old to be Girl Scouts,
pushing past our teens,
but still we locked the double doors,
stuffed our pipes and inhaled
until I felt my lungs turning black
as pirate ship sails,
ready to let any storm rip through me.
Better to travel down
into the sea's dead center,
        the room of nothing but weather,
        the peg-legged sailor's grave,
than to work on a barge at anchor,
like my mother who looked up and waved.
Her hands would always be chapped
and smell like halibut,
because she was not drowning,
but saved.

Asphalt

Harold "Andy" Anderson, grand
dad, you were a crack shot, tough jerky,
and so tan that all winter it seemed
you were just back from a dream
vacation. Why, if the midnight sun
burns twenty-four hours in Sweden,
are Andersons so white? You alone
browned, as you worked pouring asphalt
downtown, then steamed yourself red
at night in the full body steamer
with only your head sticking out,
like John the Baptist's, on a platter.
When I come home to Washington
in summer I drive over blacktop
that glitters darkly in the industrial
district around the Port of Seattle.
You are not there, among the warehouses
full of office supplies, but if you were alive
you'd steal me a box of pencils.
No CEO, not you, but you poured
terra so *firma* that my roads run
out of yours, Harold Anderson.

Life Ring

Near Guatemala, 1994

The ferry is made of rotting wood
chopped in a forest burning with news,
and smells of unlit passages
and of the woman next to me
who carried fifteen pounds of fish
aboard on her head. Her neck
is a trunk, straight and thick.
Destination: Puerto Barrios,
but between here and there
are huge swells and a pink
sky heavy with stars that gleam
like drips of milk on a sow's teats.
The hull shivers and creaks.
There's no dinghy on this ferry,
and the shore is submerged like a gator,
not moving but breathing.
In calmer weather the strong
necked woman would work
on deck, cleaning her fish.
But tonight she dozes. Her dream
is green: she's ten, trapping
tarantulas with a younger
brother who grew up to disappear.
His knees are fresh knobs.
The garden is deep in webs.
If I could speak her language
(but I can't) she'd open her eyes,
pull out her brother's picture and coax him
halfway into the light.

Synchronized Swimming

How did decay work its way into the theater of water,
the Green Lake Aqua Stadium that was clear as chlorine
all through the fifties when Marilyns, Sues, and Doreens

formed a human hula hoop of blues and greens?
The past is a bag of Wonder Bread: bright dots, trapped air,
a place that suffocates. Still, I think the sky rose like yeast

when my mother, age twelve, broke the surface of the pool
as one-tenth of an opening rose. Her legs were firm fish:
all muscle, nothing to jiggle or squish. If I could visit her

in 1956, I would brush by like a cat, my eyes fixed
on some blah boy with a buzz cut. I would ignore
her spectacular kicks. I would not betray her with a kiss.

Part Three: Garden of Forks

Doing "Theory"

I leave to various future times, but not to all,
my Garden of Forking Paths.
                                    —J.L. Borges

I took a wrong turn
into the Garden of Forks:
plunged in predawn darkness,
metallic as a Chicago subway,
wiped free of the slips and slides
of Breakfasts Past.
Hey diddle diddle, the landscape was stripped
of cow and dish and spoon,
and light leaked—guilty, milky—
from the insurmountable moon.
The forks stood, clean tin Puritans,
on geometric paths.
A structuralist would grin
at the placement of their stems.
He'd lie flat
to watch unsteady starlight palpitate
between the forks' triune upended tines.
I wandered west for hours,
but could not find even a flicker
of neon from the dissolved diner
that once slammed these forks through its dented
dishwasher, not even a shadow
of the waitress in the window,
tottering on bandages and bunions,
balancing a Denver omelet, $3.95, with its lip
of grease, its broken
circles of onion, its fine, gooey,
edible insides.

Antarctica

Written upon the signing of a multinational treaty designed to preserve Antarctica as an "unclaimed continent."

If my flat in Chicago is haunted, it's haunted
by cabbages, and maybe by a woman
whose husband held her head under the newly
installed running water as punishment for burning
dinner in 1920. It's haunted by the 20th century
creeping in with its wire bones, its closed
frontier, its bulbs and gramophones.
If there's the ghost of a frontier left,

it's in Antarctica. Maybe the woman with soaking
hair dreamed of pulling on her sweater
and heading south past Patagonia to fields
of white waves enchanted into an acropolis
of ice, where she could crash into stillness,
a caryatid in a landmass without memory,
barely brushed by the cabbage steam
and the chapped red dishwater hands of history.

Floor 19

Hyde Park Boulevard, 1994

My neighbor upstairs is all clog.
At 2 a.m. skyscrapers flood

my futon with fluorescence
as clogs clatter like codes

tapped out by a dyslexic psychic.
The offices shine all night

as Hmong women run vacuums
down halls of blinding light.

The window banks shimmer
as if the city's architecture,

revolving doors, Swedish
finish floors, were painfully gaining

the power of not-quite-human
speech, its phonemes just out

of reach, like notes above high C,
the dead, or lottery money.

      ***

In my dream Zelda Fitzgerald
flees her asylum fire

as her lithium clears for a split
second and her tongue unties

like a straitjacket sleeve:
at last she can tell the story of a city

burning down, a birthday cake
about to be blown out, and how dark

the dark feels that follows
with its welter of wished wishes.

Century of Privacy

I'd pay double
my current rent
if I could move
out of the chipped concrete
and into the architectural,
            the theoretical,
Christopher Wren's
bird's eye view of the blueprint:
not the dome,
but the dome before it began,
St. Paul's when it occupied
the kingdom of geometry,
its great hall airy with solitude
and impossibility.

            ***

Hang it all, Christopher Wren:
rooms are not pure
protection from the elements.

> *As I was going to St. Paul's*
> *I walked into doors,*
> *I walked into walls.*
> *I hit my head*
> *and it started to snow,*
> *and I knew that I wasn't in England.*

The twentieth century
would have been the century of privacy,
if anyone could live alone
for one-tenth of a second.
But nobody can. Not even the old
man who runs the elevator

at the Space Needle in Seattle, who swears
he hasn't seen his sons in twenty years,
except he brings them up
every day as he works the elevator,
repeating their names,
Stephen and *Aaron*,
to strangers.

Swan Lake

for C.

The night is loose as a dancer's joints
so I trip on my coat, but we're graceful

swans, you and I, when we finally strip
off our clothes and leap into Lake Michigan,

risking sexually transmitted hypothermia.
The night bends backwards

like a broken elbow and takes us over
the cusp of pain into an ether

where other people deal with life
(slather on Oil of Olay, give birth)

and we're free for sex with no strings
hooked to our backs. This is real flying,

not like the stage Peter Pan: we can lift
ourselves over the waves with our hands.

White

Chicago, 1994

Chris the UFOlogist
wears a shirt the color of stars
to Thanksgiving dinner,
and brings stacks of UFO testimonials
to read over coffee and pie:
An Indianapolis shrink claims captors
removed his fingernails;
Rick B. of Maine swears he was sober
when reptoids dismembered his cow;
Ms. Julia Cloche fell three million feet
and landed unbruised in a field of alfalfa.
Abductees report somnambulism,
bouts of ESP,
and a diminished fear of death.
Chris sips his coffee
and says, "Other worlds won't touch you
unless you're receptive to risk."
That nixes me, since I'm nervous
taking the South Side Local after dark
because it runs past Projects and torched cars,
past knots of women I'll never talk to
and who will never talk to me,
and yet I'm flooded by an urge
to be snatched by aliens and ferried to a star
as if UFOs are safer
than public transportation
in a city where the language of race
abducts us
and tells us who we are.

Weather at Ten

for H.

*The circle that rests closed in itself and, being substance,
holds its moments, is the immediate and therefore not
perplexing relation.*
    —G.W.F. Hegel, *Preface to Phenomenology*

It has been snowing since before
the beginning of winter.
If my ears were shells,
I'd hear the ocean, frozen

in mid-roar. Instead I hear bells:
on 55th, the Unitarians
have hired a bell-ringer
from the Netherlands

who booms out Bach,
though once he rang
Ring-a-ring o' roses,
recalling the circles children

form to rehearse death-by-pox.
But mostly he plays Bach,
as if his notes were steps
to steady us as we cross the ice,

though music's neither boat nor bridge.
Six blocks away from me,
in Harper Library,
you read yourself invisible,

burying your eyes in Hegel.
All the bulbs in the yard
are frozen solid,
like millionaires entombed in ice

waiting to melt back into life.
Our tulips will be freaks if they bloom.
Even when I sleep in your bed
I am not in your room.

Sunflowers

Did the ice age rev up slowly,
a cold ring numbing the nub
of the brontosaurus's tail,

or did it blow in fast,
sending pterodactyls hailing
down dead in droves?

My ex turned ex slowly,
vanishing over the winter
like a Cheshire cat,

leaving a guilty smile
under a guilty hat. Grr,
I craved an extra row

of teeth to gnash, reaching
back to the bit of gene
we share with sharks.

I circled the dead yard
until summer fell full,
its heat cupping sunflowers

as they sprouted from seeds
dropped by long-gone crows;
until all those sunflowers

turned over-the-top
yellow, heavy as plates
loaded with leftovers

that taste better the morning
after dinner, when the cook
eats alone in the garden.

Not Speaking

I ought to hand you a plate of dirt,
but instead, when we pass on the street,

I feel myself sprouting ghost-limbs
until I'm spidery as Kali, and part

of me hands over a counter-solar
bouquet: night-shade, Mars roses, the tulip's

dark chamber. After St. Helens blew,
floating boulders dotted the Pacific,

and the sun set blue. If I "say it with flowers,"
as the FTD Florists advise,

what can I say to you? Crocus pocus,
the sky is turning inside out like an exploding

volcano and all of the blooms in my arms
were ripped from the garden we grew.

The Man without a Middle

after a painting by René Magritte

"Monsieur, your ribcage
    is a birdcage."

"Yes, well, my heart felt imprisoned
in my ribs, so I cut it out,
like a zealous saint,
and buried it at Père Lachiase,
where it sprouted a maze of foxgloves.
Since then, I have taken in boarders:
pigeons, and the occasional hen.
I once had a teenage nightingale,
but he was worse than my erstwhile heart:
demanded six worms a day!
These pigeons, by contrast, ask nothing.
They gurgle, like water at Lourdes,
or blood from a Muslim martyr's font.
They cannot be bothered with words.
They swallow for me,
and breathe for me,
and their eyes have become my eyes.
I see a blunt world, based on food,
and I wouldn't accept my heart again:
it's poisoned with petals, it's bad for the head.
So many things are more central than love:
shiny bottle caps, for instance,
or the woman in the park near the Gare St-Lazare
(God bless her!) who scatters the bread."

Really Barely There

Sometimes love misses the mark, like a meat cleaver
      hurled at an intruder
            that lands smack
dab in the wall, and sticks there. Twenty years
      after I put my arm
            through a window at the Lion's Club picnic,
I can still see, though myopically,
          the red scar, and can still feel it at night,
             pumping and buzzing like an extra heart,
         a wren's organ, an unnatural part
of something sewn to my body. It doesn't hurt;
    it's really barely there,
        like the kind of love that hurls
           past the loved one's head without rustling
a hair—did I say this hair was dark?—a dark hair.
               Still, I want to pull my sleeves
down to my wrists and walk
        through an oak door humming,
           because if you're not sick there's no cure.
    So it's not a virus that makes that particular darkness
        disturb me, even now,
      though we only brushed accidentally,
and rode in crowded cars a few times knee to knee,
      and once a hell
             of a long time ago hiked 5,000 feet
to a ridge where it was so cold the sun felt dead,
      and the only heat worth seeking was between our toes,
      inside of our mouths, and under our skin,
           but we did not touch.
Can lack of contact leave a scar? To regret
      would be excessive, so I feel something smaller,
   a wren's claw
      clawing me lightly, the way dark hair might brush
        my cheek
          in the split second just before sleep.

Part Four: Distance Learning

Gossip

People open up like doors
onto the blowing prairie

with its gorse, its fever ticks,
and the tricks a twister plays:

setting a child in a buffalo wallow
and her crib in a willow upriver.

People open up and the whoosh
of their weather untethers

dark lilies, a moon so full
it splits in two, a cold spell

that drives mice into the heart
of the hay. Maps map zip

on this frontier. The world
is aswirl in Wile E. Coyote

fake roads. Sunflowers
spin like Ezekiel's wheels,

like doorknobs on portals
swinging to let in Lord

knows what: a dangerous
pollen count, airborne toads,

the sense of being stunned
and swept off your own land.

Teen Idol, Found O.D.'d

You were a marvelous infant,
a golden Aussie egg,

your falsetto destined to saturate
fern bars worldwide. You grew

to hear yourself pour out doors
on Dodge City Drive, and your reverb

washed over the mermaids in Santa
Maria dei Miracoli. You said yes

to everything, a porous stone
in Eden, and poppies filled the sky

until it rained fields you cooked white
in a spoon over Zippo light.

Andy Gibb, you're gone
from the radiowaves. You surfed

out of your skin and got caught
with Callisto (Zeus's lover-turned-bear)

in the constellations: remote
echoes of earth that lack

the click of ursine claws,
Farrah Fawcett hair,

K-Tel's soundtrack of "The '70s,"
the halo of common air.

A Diary in the Strict Sense of the Term

That spring there were alligators in Green Lake.
The Seattle Aquarium rescued them
and nursed them as their skin dissolved,

eyes creamed, and Bayou smiles grew fixed
as Ponce de León's fake map.
During the days before they died,

I sat stone-still in a river of reading,
hooked on the *Seattle Times*,
jobless, enclosed in my boyfriend's kitchen

with its fridge full of Diet Coke.
Zoologists deemed the gators dumped pets,
and I pictured them born in a spit-warm

bathtub, staring at tile, their stub legs limp,
swallowing bits of boiled egg.
How did the first shock of Green Lake feel?

Like death, but quivering and limned
in milfoil, spears of sun, the lick of wind
through waves, a deep cold, a reason to swim.

Sugar

My five-cent gummi bear's dyed deep red
by chemicals mysterious to me
as the As and Bs of blood.
Is it kin to the Hart's Pass grizzly who mauled
two backpackers in their dome?

Some Salish say human and animal bodies
generate tiny twins
who can enter a sleeping enemy's house
or tent, or ear, or open mouth,
and kill them. I chew the bear

slowly and picture my fifty
year old father shrunk down to age six,
in Sarpsborg, Norway, being slipped
his first chocolate ever
by an occupying Nazi

who later shot the schoolteacher
during one winter when people were stretching
their flour with bark from trees.
My dad bit down and reeled into heaven.
It was that kind of sweet.

A Bee Egg Hops

The house on Bergen Street is deep in shock.
It is—I am—painted white.
I sit at the table,
trying to write a sentence,
keeping not just the words but the letters
in alphabetical order.
It's harder than I thought;
my best is A BEE EGG HOPS.
Death makes sense, but not to me.
To me it's Wonderland:
a thin man no one can see
calling my grandfather "client" and shooting
preservatives into his groin.
If it were 1850,
my mother and I would wash the body
with soap that we made from fat.
We'd tie his arms to his sides
and fill the room with roses. As is,
he's a turned-off T.V.,
his frequency traveling above the treeline,
higher than any prime number.
We did not expect this: we are a lucky family,
tossing eggs in the egg toss longer
than anyone else at the neighborhood picnic
and catching them gently.
Our old world name begins with Ø,
a letter that comes after Z,
as if in the aftershock I—we—
could lapse into automatic writing,
into palindromes like my Grandma Anna,
circling back from Z
with no sense of an ending: AnnA, AnnA AnnA.
But hell is jabber, and I know my grandfather
tossed himself out of the world like an egg:

gently.

Electricity

Great-grandmother Signe
said it: *God is electricity*.
In 1903, just off the boat
from Christiania, Norway,
she watched, fascinated, as Topsy

the Coney Island elephant
was electrocuted: an animal
the size of a small landmass
falling far from India
with no other elephants afoot
      to cover the corpse in grass.

When Franklin slipped
a key on his kite
he unlocked a door in the sky
to find, not the portals
of heaven, but earthly power,

touchy and bright, like Signe
who raised her daughters
to use the right fork at dinner
and to dress better than the neighbors.
Generations generate

back to back like batteries.
This is not memory,
it's immortality:
the blood's acidity,
the rub of ribs on ribs.

My nerves draw on her surge
like elephants who return
each year to their forbears' bones,
honoring—or mourning—
their own genetic code.
     When I was eight,

Signe poured me black
coffee as we walked in circles,
putting Thanksgiving together.
I wanted to open a secret drawer
full of scrambled silverware,
     krof, fienk, opso—

to fly to pieces, to speak in riddles
Signe couldn't follow,
but the coffee jolted me
around the dining room,
and I set the table correctly:
     fork, knife, spoon.

May Day, 1989

The tulip tree doesn't know when to stop: it sheds
      its petals, pink pink pink, yin without yang,

the pale tongues of girls, snipped and scattered.
      Their silence is bloodless; I walk through it,

kicking up scent, en route to exercise class.
      Why do I want to keep my figure, my hour

glass with its falling stream of sand? Surely
      there are grander shapes: down by Lake Union,

a statue of Lenin, salvaged from a Siberian
      town square, stabs one finger in the air,

pointing at something—some Hegelian dialectic—
      that has escaped us. History is birds flying,

it is the dialect of migration. Each spring,
      the tulip tree blooms again, and the robins

return, brown and sane. Oh, but our eyes
      play tricks, comrade: everything has changed.

Distance Learning

ca. 1992

They answered an ad,
FINISH SCHOOL BY CORRESPONDENCE,
so now I'm making six bucks an hour
teaching Practical English
to Benjy the Seventh Day Adventist who sells
Awake in front of Dunkin' Donuts;
and to Annabella the third generation
contortionist in a one-ring circus;
and to Tim from Nome whose stick dance
makes fish rush to the surface of the sea.
Our textbook, revised in 1956,
calls English a "tool" as if it could conk Satan
over the head as he slunk out of Dunkin' Donuts.
Its rules are iron-clad, a chain of Is before Es
not bendable like the bones in a young body,
not sprung from monks and slaves and thieves.
I'm required to teach the text straight,
as if on a cold night outside Nome
an Athabaskan could smoke
salmon with wood from a grammar tree.
My students are remote as astrophysics:
stars and particle waves, the phenomenon
of light traveling over distance,
constructed from equations I can't trace
although our textbook ventures that someday
Americans will send a man into space.

Ars Poetica,
or Rough Crossing

Part the lunar ocean, Moses,
and you'll find not fish but ice: the night's

aesthetic centerpiece supports no life,
no red plankton, no crush of Israelites.

The moon was a dead white disc the night
the ferry *Elwha* half-sank. My neck

snapped back as we lodged in a sandbar,
and the captain stubbed out his joint,

and a child screamed Kim Kim Kim
—her own name—and the vending machine

tipped over, scattering change. *Ars poetica:*
what are these two words but frozen

stones from the lunar sea,
from a language remote as Virgil is to me?

And yet every passenger wanted to write
—if not an epic then at least a note—

this was clear from the way they fastened
their orange flotation jackets.

And yes, every passenger (plus four dogs)
was saved. Once back on solid ground,

my walk broke into a run,
and the moon came alive

and it spoke in Latin. *Ars poetica*, it said,
which means *the promised land is ink on paper:*
       tame the sea, cross over, write to remember.

Crossing to the Coast

At 6 a.m. it's snowing in Selah,
and a man with a bird
nest beard spreads out his map

at the Denny's and draws,
between bites of bear claw,
a route West over the Cascade mountains.

He tells me to keep my eyes
glued to the road. Christ,
unfolded maps are hard to refold.

They loll like accordions,
as if cartography were so wobbly
that we woke every day in a new country

full of new chords, and we do,
as if the Cascade passes,
Chinook, Stevens, Snoqualmie,

were impassable, and they are—
almost. As I start climbing, the FM goes,
and I drive through fog,

chains strapped to my wheels,
barely remembering how the knob feels
that opens my parents' door.

After Enumclaw
the radio rebuilds its brain,
finding words for the weather,

but as the landscape grows more familiar
it grows more strange,
like my mother's fox fur

that fits me like a dream,
with its cut-off paws and its half-wild scent:
no nails, no nerves, no secrets.

Empire Builder

Chicago-Seattle, 1995

Where do the buffalo roam? Once,
the West was a playfield

for pioneers, who saw money bleeding
from the great creatures' ears.

They shot them by the million
from this route, so now it's tame:

a country of doves and sage.
My husband spotted a buffalo,

or did he dream it? I don't know.
The past is a closed drawer.

Maybe there really were angels
circling the Great Salt Lake

in Brigham Young's day,
but their wings are snipped at the root

and folded, private as underwear.
They won't block the track. No

turning back: tonight, we'll pass
Glacier Park in the dark,

on a trestle so high the sleeping
bears won't rouse. Remote

as a meteor traversing Ursa Major,
we'll push west to Seattle,

to our house, to our bed in the red
cedar basement, to our St. Francis

night light burning with power
from rivers full of dead salmon

trapped by dams. St. Francis's feet
and fingers flood the room with faux fire:

this is how we live, with our bones
in blood, at the end of the empire.

Uses of Enchantment

It is therefore that I would have woman lay aside all
thought such as she habitually cherishes, of being taught
and led by men. I would have her, like the Indian girl,
dedicate herself to the sun.
                                        —Margaret Fuller, 1845

I'm pulling weeds
in the Woodmont Beach
house garden,
while in Puget Sound,
beyond the chaos of roses and peas,
sunset ignites
bonfires underwater.
The flames spread.
The ballad of the dead
is sung beneath the surface in slow
sync with anemones,
saturated by the deep
pull of a story
that's truer than zoology,
but seems strange
as a speaking salmon,
or a seal with a scarlet pelt.
The story explains
that though dusk will always rekindle
under Puget Sound,
my grandmother will never swim
up from under death
clenching her golden teeth.
All that's left is a handful
of enchanted seeds
that she packed into the calcium
spines of my mother and me,

that force us upward
like stalks from beans
driven crazy in love with the sun.

Photo by Mardi Mileham

Angela Sorby was born and raised in Seattle, graduated from the University of Washington, and received her Ph.D. from the University of Chicago. She has been the recipient of a "Discovery" /*The Nation* Award and has appeared in *Best American Poetry*. She currently lives in Oregon with her husband and son and teaches at Linfield College.

Mekeel McBride is the author of four books of poetry, most recently, from Carnegie Mellon University Press, *Red Letter Days* and *Wind of the White Dresses*.